GREAT SOURCE

Test Achiever

Mastering Standardized Tests

Grade 1

Test preparation for reading,
language arts, and mathematics

GReaT SouRCe
EDUCATION GROUP
A Houghton Mifflin Company

Design and production by Publicom, Inc., Acton, Massachusetts

Printed in the United States of America

International Standard Book Number: 0-669-46456-2

7 8 9 10 11 12 13 14 15 16 - HS - 08 07 06 05 04 03

URL address: http://www.greatsource.com/

Pretest

READING: Sounds and Letters

Sample

A.

pail   last   sun   late
○   ○   ○   ○

1.

mop   ride   pet   door
○   ○   ○   ○

2.

drip   free   the   try
○   ○   ○   ○

Sample

B.

cap   time   kind   sit
○   ○   ○   ○

3.

bug   lot   gold   lake
○   ○   ○   ○

Go On

4.

send   star   most   nice
○   ○   ○   ○

5.

met   thumb   hot   both
○   ○   ○   ○

(Sample)

C.

tug   song   dig   seed
○   ○   ○   ○

6.

pull   luck   ship   pack
○   ○   ○   ○

7.

wet   where   deep   head
○   ○   ○   ○

8.

cat   drop   store   road
○   ○   ○   ○

Stop

Pretest

READING: Vocabulary

Sample

| A. | song ○ | road ○ | bike ○ | food ○ |

| 1. | game ○ | home ○ | king ○ | story ○ |

| 2. | push ○ | mix ○ | leave ○ | hold ○ |

| 3. | tent ○ | clown ○ | mouse ○ | trick ○ |

| 4. | surprise ○ | street ○ | cloud ○ | breakfast ○ |

| 5. | turtle ○ | zoo ○ | bear ○ | worker ○ |

Stop

Sample

B. Linda has blue eyes. Tim's eyes are _____.

- ○ fast
- ○ green
- ○ hot

8. My old coat is too small. I need a _____ one.

- ○ slow
- ○ new
- ○ funny

6. Dennis came into the room and sat down on the _____.

- ○ park
- ○ friend
- ○ chair

9. Meg left her books on the _____.

- ○ table
- ○ morning
- ○ bone

7. Amy looked out the _____ and saw a rainbow.

- ○ window
- ○ show
- ○ winter

10. I think lunch is ready. I can _____ the soup.

- ○ smell
- ○ clean
- ○ laugh

Stop

Pretest

READING: Comprehension

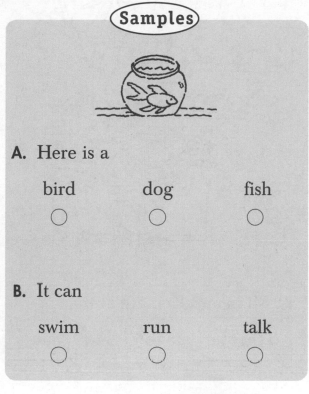

A. Here is a

bird	dog	fish
○	○	○

B. It can

swim	run	talk
○	○	○

1. Tommy is pulling a

book	wagon	plant
○	○	○

2. It is filled with

frogs	wood	toys
○	○	○

3. Lin sits at the

water	table	basket
○	○	○

4. She is going to

eat	walk	jump
○	○	○

Go On →

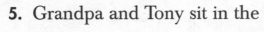

5. Grandpa and Tony sit in the

    boat   truck   house

    ◯   ◯   ◯

8. Mimi and Ken are at the

    school   zoo   fair

    ◯   ◯   ◯

6. They ride in the

    grass   tree   water

    ◯   ◯   ◯

9. They will play a

    game   trick   meal

    ◯   ◯   ◯

7. They will go across the

    street   country   lake

    ◯   ◯   ◯

10. Mimi wants to win a

    pet   prize   box

    ◯   ◯   ◯

Stop

Samples

Nick

Neva got a new puppy. The puppy's name was Nick. First, Neva gave the puppy some food. Then she dropped a ball on the floor. The puppy ran after the ball.

C. This story tells about

○ a girl named Nick

○ a new puppy

○ a funny friend

D. What does Neva give to the puppy?

○ some food

○ a bed

○ two shoes

Tree Frogs

Most tree frogs are very small. They are about as long as your finger. Tree frogs are not like other frogs. Most tree frogs live in trees. They do not live in water. Tree frogs are green or brown. They can change their color to hide from other animals.

11. A tree frog is about as long as

○ a foot

○ a hand

○ a finger

12. Tree frogs are not like other frogs because they

○ swim

○ live in trees

○ are green or brown

Go On →

Stan Goes for a Walk

One day a mouse named Stan found some cheese.

"I will take this cheese to my friend, Lisa," Stan said to himself. "She will like this cheese."

Stan walked to Lisa's house. Then he knocked on the door. But no one answered.

"Oh, well," said Stan. He sat down. "Lisa would not like this cheese anyway."

13. What did Stan do first?

○ He found some cheese.

○ He knocked on a door.

○ He sat down.

14. Where did Stan go?

○ into his home

○ to the store

○ to Lisa's house

15. Why didn't Lisa eat the cheese?

○ She was not hungry.

○ She was not at home.

○ She did not like cheese.

16. What will Stan do next?

○ eat the cheese

○ knock on the door

○ go home

Stop

Pretest

READING: Listening

○ ○ ○

1.

○ ○ ○

2.

○ ○ ○

3.

○ ○ ○

Go On →

4.

○   ○   ○

5.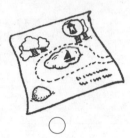

○   ○   ○

6. RIGHT    UP   LEFT

○   ○   ○

7.

○   ○   ○

8.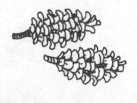

○   ○   ○

Stop

Pretest

LANGUAGE ARTS: Usage

Sample

A. His bike _____.

- ○ and my bike
- ○ is red
- ○ with a bell

1. Two boys _____ into the school.

- ○ ran
- ○ runs
- ○ running

2. Max has two _____.

- ○ dog
- ○ dogs

3. My dad _____.

- ○ works at night
- ○ and my mom
- ○ with black hair

4. _____ to the zoo.

- ○ A monkey
- ○ Many kids
- ○ We went

5. Kara is the _____ girl in our class.

- ○ tall
- ○ taller
- ○ tallest

6. My sister _____ you.

- ○ like
- ○ likes

7. Sally did not go to school because _____ was sick.

- ○ he
- ○ they
- ○ she

Stop

Sample

B. Tom can read.

- ○ Read Tom can?
- ○ Tom read can?
- ○ Can Tom read?

Sample

C. ○ All day at the beach.

- ○ I love the sun.
- ○ Sand in my shirt and my hair.

---

8. The bird is blue.

- ○ Bird is the blue?
- ○ Is the bird blue?
- ○ Blue is the bird?

11. ○ We rode our bikes.

- ○ Waited at the stop sign on the corner.
- ○ The big red car.

---

9. Tina will go home.

- ○ Will Tina go home?
- ○ Go home will Tina?
- ○ Home will go Tina?

12. ○ So many pretty flowers.

- ○ Bees like flowers.
- ○ Red roses and yellow roses.

---

10. The clouds are white.

- ○ White are the clouds?
- ○ The white clouds are?
- ○ Are the clouds white?

13. ○ Mom tells the best stories.

- ○ A long, funny one.
- ○ Two surprises at the end.

Stop

Pretest

LANGUAGE ARTS: Mechanics

Sample

A.
- ○   Uncle Manny came to
- ○ visit. he always brings a
- ○ present for me.

1.
- ○   Ted's birthday is on
- ○ monday. My birthday is at
- ○ the end of July.

2.
- ○   Cole and i went to the
- ○ zoo. We saw a lion climb
- ○ into a big tree.

3.
- ○   what is your name?
- ○ Dad says that you live in
- ○ the house next to ours.

4.
- ○   Mr. Otis calls to his
- ○ dog, rex. Every night
- ○ they go for a long walk.

5.
- ○   Today is the last day
- ○ of the summer. We will go
- ○ to school on august 23.

Stop

B. (Sample)

- ○ Birds eat seeds
- ○ Where is the bird?
- ○ What color is it.

C. (Sample)

you	open	windoe
○	○	○

6.

- ○ I have a pet snake?
- ○ My snake is named Slim?
- ○ Do you want to see it?

9.

hear	techer	said
○	○	○

10.

arund	park	today
○	○	○

7.

- ○ Bob has a new toy.
- ○ It is a green truck?
- ○ He rides the truck in the house

11.

woman	drives	buz
○	○	○

8.

- ○ Do you watch TV?
- ○ Where is the TV.
- ○ I like to watch it sometimes

12.

thoze	toys	table
○	○	○

Stop

Pretest

Sample

A. I have my own garden.
First I get the soil ready.

_____

○ The sun is hot today.

○ Then I plant some seeds.

○ I like carrots best.

1. Jan has a wagon.
The wagon is red.

_____

○ She likes her wagon.

○ I have a wagon, too.

○ Do you have a wagon?

2. Mom needs a new car.
She likes yellow best.

_____

○ We ride to school.

○ What color is your car?

○ Mom gets a yellow car.

Our family went to the city.
We rode on a train.
The city is very busy.
We saw lots of people.
Then we went to a store.

_____

3. ○ The train went very fast.

○ I like riding the train better
than riding the bus.

○ The store was filled with toys.

4. ○ to make you laugh

○ to tell about a trip to the city

○ to tell how to get to the city

Stop

15

B. (Sample)

- ○ cat
- ○ bird
- ○ dog

6.

- ○ green
- ○ pink
- ○ yellow

5.

- ○ tent
- ○ house
- ○ cabin

7.

- ○ sister
- ○ mother
- ○ father

Contents

1. Trees 1
2. Flowers 5
3. Fruits 9
4. Vegetables 12

8.

- ○ page 1
- ○ page 5
- ○ page 9

9.

- ○ Trees
- ○ Flowers
- ○ Fruits

Stop

Pretest

MATHEMATICS: Concepts

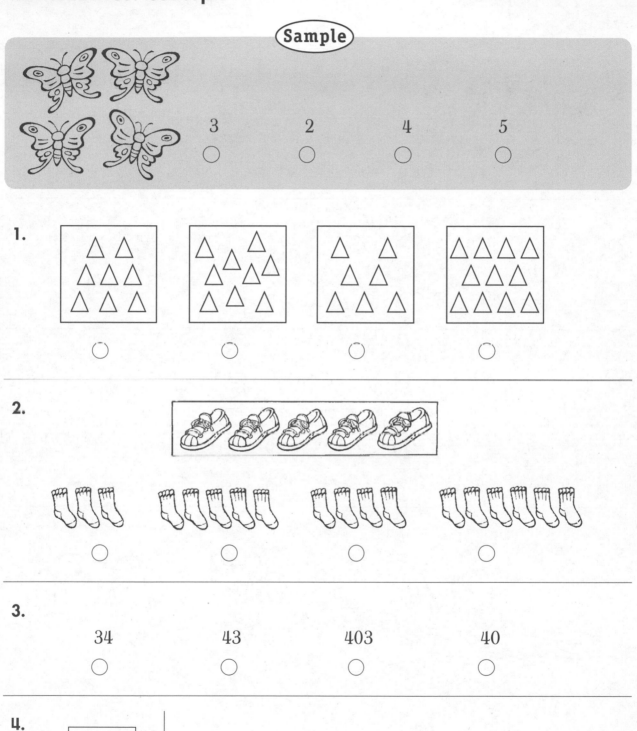

Sample

3   2   4   5
○   ○   ○   ○

1.
○   ○   ○   ○

2.
○   ○   ○   ○

3.
34   43   403   40
○   ○   ○   ○

4.
10 | one   nine   seven   ten
○   ○   ○   ○

Go On

5.

6	4	7	8
○	○	○	○

6.

5	22	31	32
○	○	○	○

7.

18	21	30	20
○	○	○	○

8.

25	30	35		45

36	40	39	50
○	○	○	○

9.

    ○   ○   ○   ○

Go On →

10.

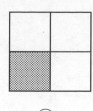 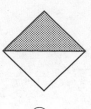 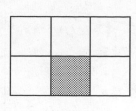

      ○   ○   ○   ○

11.

$$5 + 1 = 6$$

$5 + 6 = 11$ $6 + 1 = 7$ $6 - 1 = 5$ $5 - 1 = 4$

    ○   ○   ○   ○

12.

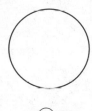

    ○   ○   ○   ○

13.

    ○   ○   ○   ○

14.

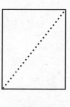

    ○   ○   ○   ○

Go On →

15.

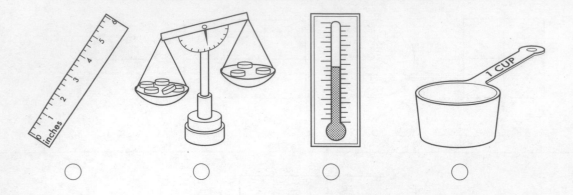

○   ○   ○   ○

16.

25¢   27¢   17¢   32¢

○   ○   ○   ○

17.

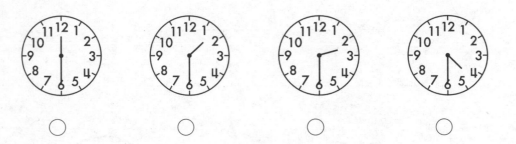

○   ○   ○   ○

18. BOOKMARK BOOKMARK

5   6   7   8

○   ○   ○   ○

Stop

Pretest

MATHEMATICS: Computation

Sample

4	5	6	N
○	○	○	○

4.

21	22	23	N
○	○	○	○

1.

5	6	7	N
○	○	○	○

5.

3	4	5	N
○	○	○	○

2.

9	11	37	N
○	○	○	○

6.

0	1	8	N
○	○	○	○

3.

12	14	15	N
○	○	○	○

7.

2	3	4	N
○	○	○	○

Go On

8.

$$\begin{array}{r} 3 \\ +\ 5 \\ \hline \end{array}$$

7	8	9	N
○	○	○	○

12.

$$\begin{array}{r} 31 \\ +\ 15 \\ \hline \end{array}$$

16	24	46	N
○	○	○	○

9.

$$\begin{array}{r} 6 \\ +\ 8 \\ \hline \end{array}$$

12	15	16	N
○	○	○	○

13.

$$\begin{array}{r} 8 \\ -\ 2 \\ \hline \end{array}$$

5	6	10	N
○	○	○	○

10.

$$12 + 0 =$$

11	12	13	N
○	○	○	○

14.

$$\begin{array}{r} 17 \\ -\ 9 \\ \hline \end{array}$$

11	10	9	N
○	○	○	○

11.

$$\begin{array}{r} 4 \\ 5 \\ +\ 9 \\ \hline \end{array}$$

13	14	18	N
○	○	○	○

15.

$$25 - 14 =$$

11	12	39	N
○	○	○	○

Stop

22

Pretest

MATHEMATICS: Problem Solving

Sample

9

2

5
○

6
○

7
○

11
○

1.

$8 + 5 = \square$
○

$5 - 8 = \square$
○

$5 + 8 = \square$
○

$8 - 5 = \square$
○

2.

4
○

5
○

7
○

10
○

3.

10
○

13
○

14
○

17
○

ч.

1
○

2
○

3
○

5
○

Go On ➝

	3
	4
	2
	7

5.

9	14	16	17
○	○	○	○

6.

○	○	○	○

7.

5	6	7	8
○	○	○	○

8.

○	○	○	○

9.

$6	$7	$8	$9
○	○	○	○

10.

38 inches	39 inches	40 inches	41 inches
○	○	○	○

Stop

Reading

PRACTICE 1 • Letter Sounds

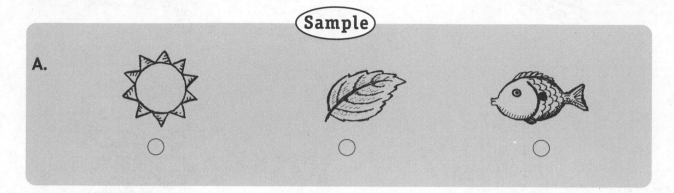

Sample

A.

Tips and Reminders

- Listen carefully to the word your teacher says.

- Say the name of each picture softly to yourself.

PRACTICE

1.

○   ○   ○

2.

○   ○   ○

Go On

3.

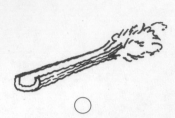  

○ ○ ○

4.

  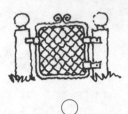

○ ○ ○

5.

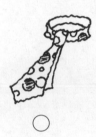  

○ ○ ○

6.

○ ○ ○

Stop

Sample

B.

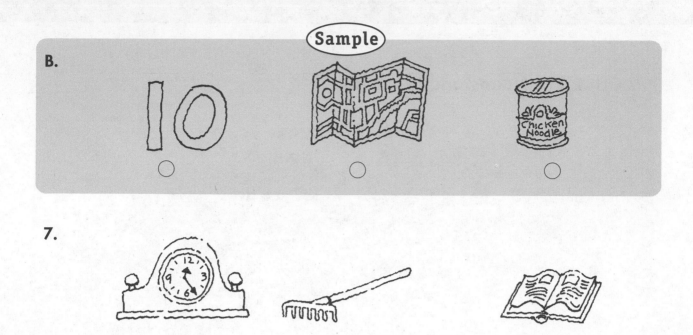

7.

8.

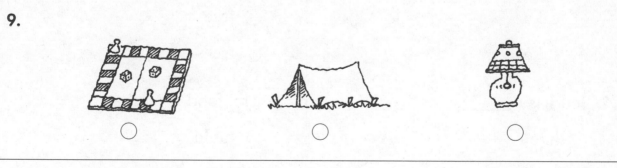

9.

10.

Stop

Language Arts

Samples

A.

Sam has a red _____.

◯ hat

◯ hats

B.

I see two _____.

◯ duck

◯ ducks

Tips and Reminders

• Try each word in the sentence.

• Pick the one that sounds right.

PRACTICE

1. Mom made five _____.

   ◯ cake

   ◯ cakes

2. Jed has a _____.

   ◯ kite

   ◯ kites

3. We saw a black _____.

   ◯ snake

   ◯ snakes

4. Dad got four small _____.

   ◯ tree

   ◯ trees

5. The food is on that _____.

   ◯ table

   ◯ tables

6. Did you tie both _____?

   ◯ shoe

   ◯ shoes

Stop

Samples

C. Leo is my brother.

- ○ He
- ○ She
- ○ They

D. The dogs run all day.

- ○ It
- ○ We
- ○ They

7. My sister is late.

- ○ He
- ○ She
- ○ Her

10. Jim and I played a game.

- ○ He
- ○ You
- ○ We

8. Those flowers are pretty.

- ○ They
- ○ We
- ○ It

11. My dad works in the park.

- ○ She
- ○ He
- ○ Him

9. The school is closed today.

- ○ He
- ○ It
- ○ They

12. That truck is big!

- ○ It
- ○ He
- ○ She

Stop

Mathematics

PRACTICE 3 • Whole Number Concepts

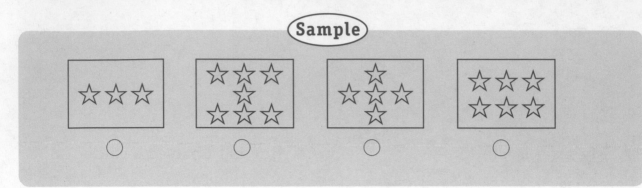

Tips and Reminders

- Listen carefully.
- Look at all the answer choices before you choose an answer.

PRACTICE

1.

17	72	20	27
○	○	○	○

2.

○   ○   ○   ○

Go On

3.

five   eight   nine   ten
○   ○   ○   ○

4.

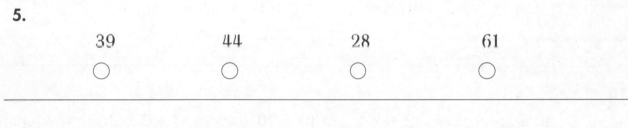

○   ○   ○   ○

5.

39   44   28   61
○   ○   ○   ○

6.

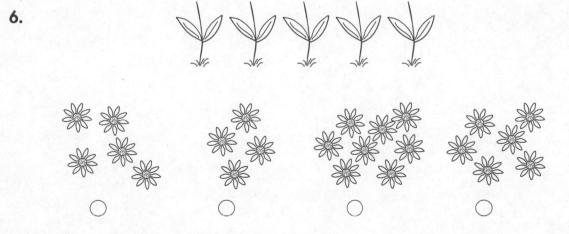

○   ○   ○   ○

Go On →

7.

20	25	31	18
○	○	○	○

8.

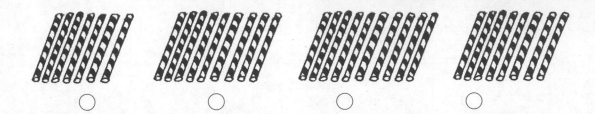

○	○	○	○

9.

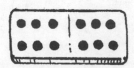

ten	twelve	six	eight
○	○	○	○

10.

10 + 2	12 + 2	10 + 10 + 2	5 + 5 + 10
○	○	○	○

Stop

32

Reading

Sample

A.   come   draw   ride   more
           ○   ○   ○   ○

Tips and Reminders

- Say each word softly to yourself.
- Watch out for words with the same ending sound.

PRACTICE

1.   best   when   stay   very
           ○   ○   ○   ○

2.    make   bed   black   late
           ○   ○   ○   ○

3.    time   back   sit   start
           ○   ○   ○   ○

4.   where   child   car   each
           ○   ○   ○   ○

Stop

Sample

B.   bell   kite   take   cab
      ○   ○   ○   ○

Tips and Reminders

• Say each word softly to yourself.

• Watch out for words with the same beginning sound.

PRACTICE

5.

all   why   like   wide
○   ○   ○   ○

6.

the   some   mud   camp
○   ○   ○   ○

7.

love   call   old   trick
○   ○   ○   ○

8.

my   then   both   mom
○   ○   ○   ○

Stop

Language Arts

PRACTICE 5 • Verbs

Samples

A. She <u>say</u> hello to me.

- ○ says
- ○ saying
- ○ The way it is

B. The boy <u>rides</u> his bike.

- ○ riding
- ○ ride
- ○ The way it is

Tips and Reminders

- Try each answer choice in the sentence.
- Choose the one that sounds right.

PRACTICE

1. Dad <u>make</u> a cake.

- ○ making
- ○ is making
- ○ The way it is

2. Polly <u>swims</u> in the pond every day.

- ○ swimmed
- ○ is swimming
- ○ The way it is

3. That horse <u>are</u> black.

- ○ is
- ○ were
- ○ The way it is

4. We <u>seen</u> a rainbow.

- ○ sees
- ○ saw
- ○ The way it is

Go On

5. Mary <u>sings</u> a song to us last night.

- ○ sang
- ○ singing
- ○ The way it is

6. We <u>stopped</u> at the store on our way home.

- ○ stops
- ○ stopping
- ○ The way it is

7. It <u>rains</u> all day yesterday.

- ○ rained
- ○ is raining
- ○ The way it is

8. When <u>were</u> your birthday?

- ○ are
- ○ was
- ○ The way it is

9. The bus <u>come</u> at seven.

- ○ comes
- ○ coming
- ○ The way it is

10. Jenna <u>take</u> her dog to school.

- ○ taked
- ○ took
- ○ The way it is

11. Can we <u>play</u> a game?

- ○ plays
- ○ played
- ○ The way it is

12. Ron <u>laugh</u> at my jokes.

- ○ laughing
- ○ laughed
- ○ The way it is

Stop

Mathematics

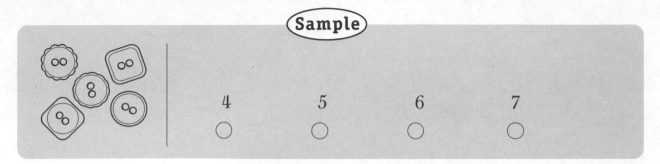

Sample

4   ○   5   ○   6   ○   7   ○

Tips and Reminders

• Listen carefully and look at the picture.

• Look at every answer choice. Then choose an answer.

PRACTICE

1.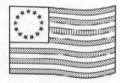

13   10   7   6
○   ○   ○   ○

2.

| 2, 4, 6, 8, ___, . . . |

7   9   10   12
○   ○   ○   ○

3.

○   ○   ○   ○

Go On

37

4.

| 31, 32, 33, ___, 35, . . . |

30   36   37   34
○   ○   ○   ○

5.

7   33   43   34
○   ○   ○   ○

6.

48   50   51   59
○   ○   ○   ○

7.

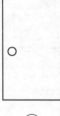

| 40 | 50 | | | | |

○   ○   ○   ○   ○   ○

○   ○   ○   ○

8.

○   ○   ○   ○

 Stop

Reading

PRACTICE 7 • Vowels

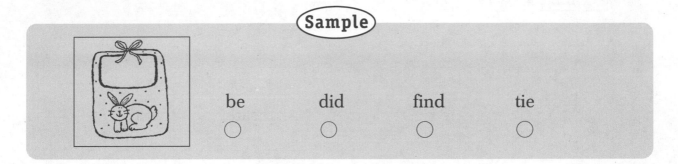

Sample

be   did   find   tie
○   ○   ○   ○

Tips and Reminders

• Read each word softly to yourself.

• Watch out for words that have the same letters but different sounds.

PRACTICE

1.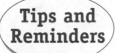

   red   not   tree   me
   ○   ○   ○   ○

2.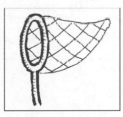

   put   turn   rule   but
   ○   ○   ○   ○

3.

   lot   now   home   top
   ○   ○   ○   ○

Go On →

4.

late ○   car ○   sat ○   park ○

5.

fed ○   met ○   read ○   friend ○

6.

mark ○   map ○   man ○   make ○

7.

out ○   you ○   nut ○   fun ○

8.

sky ○   sing ○   skip ○   still ○

Stop

Language Arts

PRACTICE 8 • Adjectives

Samples

A. Jimmy's bike is _____ than Paul's bike.

- ○ fast
- ○ faster
- ○ fastest

B. She is the _____ teacher in our school.

- ○ nice
- ○ nicer
- ○ nicest

Tips and Reminders

- Try each answer choice in the sentence.
- Choose the one that sounds right.

PRACTICE

1. This apple is the _____ one of all.

- ○ big
- ○ bigger
- ○ biggest

2. My sister is the _____ girl I know.

- ○ pretty
- ○ prettier
- ○ prettiest

3. The snow is _____ this year than it was last year.

- ○ deep
- ○ deeper
- ○ deepest

4. That noise is too _____.

- ○ loud
- ○ louder
- ○ loudest

Go On

5. Your coat is _____ than mine.

○ wet

○ wetter

○ wettest

6. It is always so _____ in the library.

○ quiet

○ quieter

○ quietest

7. This car is _____ than a truck.

○ wide

○ wider

○ widest

8. That is the _____ book I have ever read.

○ long

○ longer

○ longest

9. Today is the _____ day of the summer.

○ hot

○ hotter

○ hottest

10. Jon has _____ toys than I do.

○ many

○ more

○ most

11. Grampa is always very _____ to us.

○ kind

○ kinder

○ kindest

12. That is the _____ dog in the world!

○ fat

○ fatter

○ fattest

Mathematics

PRACTICE 9 • Using Numbers

Samples

A.

1	4	7		13

    8   9   10

    ○   ○   ○

B.

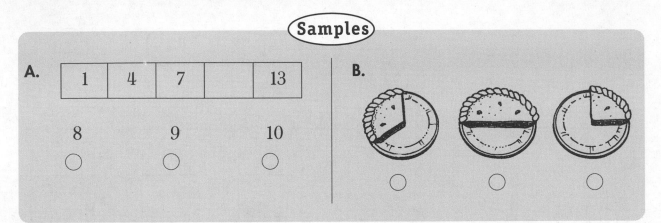

    ○   ○   ○

Tips and Reminders

- Listen carefully to the question.
- Use the pictures to help answer the questions.
- Look at every answer choice before you choose an answer.

PRACTICE

1.

   □   ☆   ♡

   ○   ○   ○

2.

6 □ 2 = 8

   +   −   =

   ○   ○   ○

Go On →

3.

10	8	?	4	2

6.

6   7   5

○   ○   ○

○   ○   ○

4.

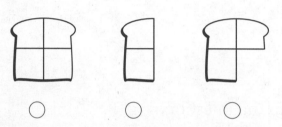

○   ○   ○

7.

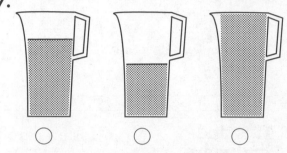

○   ○   ○

5.

$$12 \ \square \ 7 = 5$$

+   −   =

○   ○   ○

8.

$$4 + 5 \ \square \ 9$$

+   −   =

○   ○   ○

Stop

Reading

PRACTICE 10 • Sight Words

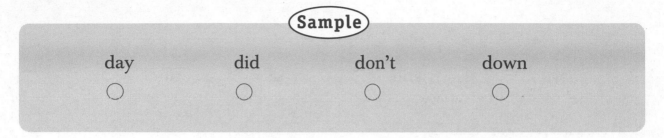

Sample

day	did	don't	down
○	○	○	○

Tips and Reminders

• Listen carefully to the word your teacher says.

• Read each word softly to yourself.

PRACTICE

1.

make	man	me	my
○	○	○	○

2.

that	they	then	thing
○	○	○	○

3.

each	eat	end	every
○	○	○	○

4.

what	with	want	was
○	○	○	○

Go On →

5.   hide   hill   him   high
     ○   ○   ○   ○

6.   found   friend   frog   find
     ○   ○   ○   ○

7.   school   show   small   still
     ○   ○   ○   ○

8.   class   clean   close   clown
     ○   ○   ○   ○

9.   nose   noise   nice   note
     ○   ○   ○   ○

10. these   those   their   there
     ○   ○   ○   ○

11. almost   already   alike   also
     ○   ○   ○   ○

12. gate   giant   given   gotten
     ○   ○   ○   ○

Stop

Language Arts

PRACTICE 11 • Sentences

Samples

A.
> Most people eat breakfast.
> In the morning.

- ○ Most people eating breakfast in the morning.
- ○ Most people eat breakfast in the morning.
- ○ The way it is

B.
> The duck swims across
> the pond.

- ○ The duck swims. Across the pond.
- ○ The duck swimming across the pond.
- ○ The way it is

Tips and Reminders

- Read every answer choice.
- A complete sentence tells who or what did something and what they did.

PRACTICE

1.
> The children ate cake. At the party.

- ○ The children ate cake at the party.
- ○ They ate it. Cake at the party.
- ○ The way it is

2.
> The clown wears funny shoes. On his feet.

- ○ The clown wears. Funny shoes on his feet.
- ○ The clown wears funny shoes on his feet.
- ○ The way it is

Go On

3. | Last night my sister. Went for a walk. |

- ○ Last night my sister went for a walk.
- ○ Last night. My sister went for a walk.
- ○ The way it is

4. | Zack plays with his new toy. |

- ○ Zack playing with his new toy.
- ○ Zack plays. With his new toy.
- ○ The way it is

5. | The little girl sings. A happy song. |

- ○ The little girl sings a happy song.
- ○ The little girl singing a happy song.
- ○ The way it is

6. | Ali likes to play. In the snow. |

- ○ Ali likes to play in the snow.
- ○ Ali liking to play in the snow.
- ○ The way it is

7. | Luis rides the bus to school. |

- ○ Luis riding the bus to school.
- ○ Luis rides the bus. To school.
- ○ The way it is

8. | A small squirrel ran. Up the tree. |

- ○ A small squirrel ran up the tree.
- ○ A small squirrel. Ran up the tree.
- ○ The way it is

Stop

48

Mathematics

PRACTICE 12 • Shapes

Sample

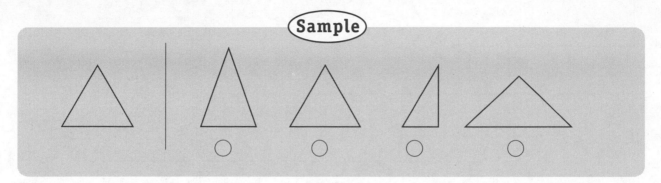

⭕   ⭕   ⭕   ⭕

Tips and Reminders

• Look at the pictures carefully.

• Check your answer.

PRACTICE

1.

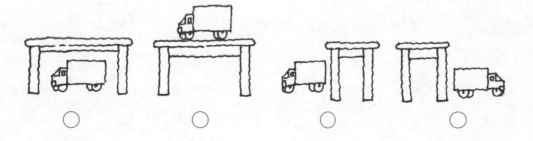

⭕   ⭕   ⭕   ⭕

2.

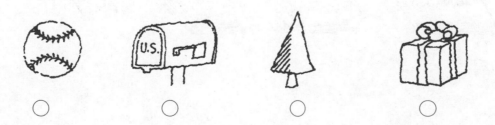

⭕   ⭕   ⭕   ⭕

Go On →

3.

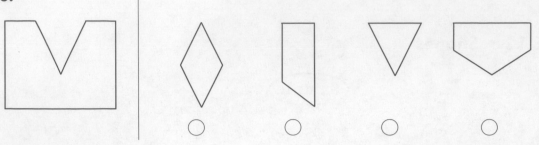

○ ○ ○ ○

4.

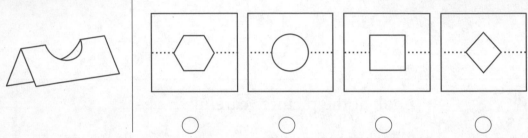

○ ○ ○ ○

5.

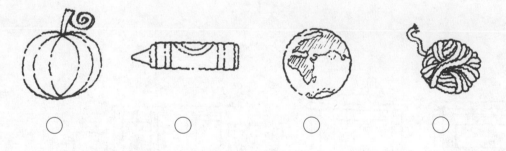

○ ○ ○ ○

6.

○ ○ ○ ○

7.

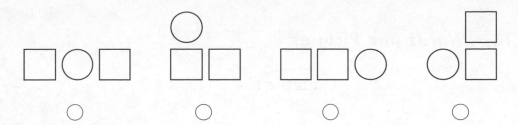

○   ○   ○   ○

8.

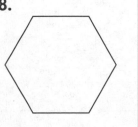

3	4	5	6
○	○	○	○

9.

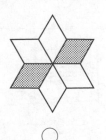

○   ○   ○   ○

10.

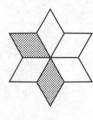 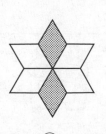

○   ○   ○   ○

Stop

Reading

PRACTICE 13 • Words and Pictures

Sample

A.

○   ○   ○

Tips and Reminders

• Listen carefully.

• Choose the picture or word that best fits the meaning.

PRACTICE

1.

○   ○   ○

2.

                    ▢

○   ○   ○

3.

○   ○   ○

Stop

Sample

B.

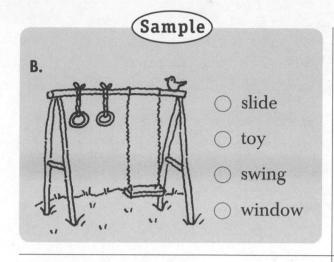

- ○ slide
- ○ toy
- ○ swing
- ○ window

4.

- ○ crawl
- ○ slide
- ○ walk
- ○ jump

5.

- ○ chair
- ○ bench
- ○ table
- ○ desk

6.

- ○ draw
- ○ paste
- ○ talk
- ○ read

7.

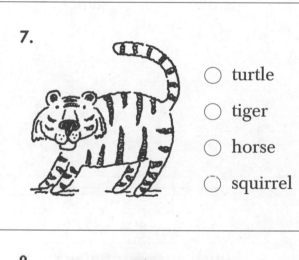

- ○ turtle
- ○ tiger
- ○ horse
- ○ squirrel

8.

- ○ cut
- ○ bake
- ○ drink
- ○ bite

Stop

(Sample)

C.

shoe	hat	coat	grass
○	○	○	○

9.

move	dance	start	give
○	○	○	○

10.

cat	snake	flower	zoo
○	○	○	○

11.

quiet	hungry	cold	dark
○	○	○	○

12.

hear	stand	move	turn
○	○	○	○

13.

stick	cave	stone	rope
○	○	○	○

Language Arts

PRACTICE 14 • Writing Sentences

Samples

A.

The children _____.

○ are hungry

○ eating

○ at the table

B.

_____ is happy.

○ Laugh and smile

○ Always

○ Grandma

Tips and Reminders

• Try each answer choice in the sentence.

• Choose the one that tells a complete idea.

PRACTICE

1. _____ walked to school.

○ Together

○ This morning

○ The two boys

2. _____ can swim.

○ All fish

○ In the pond

○ Jumping and diving

3. That horse _____.

○ in the barn

○ runs fast

○ eating grass

4. Snow _____.

○ cold and wet

○ on the ground

○ is falling outside

Stop

55

Sample

C.

Those clowns are funny.

○ Funny are those clowns?

○ Are those clowns funny?

○ Those clowns funny are?

5. I can sing.

○ Sing can I?

○ Can I sing?

○ I sing can?

6. These flowers are pretty.

○ These pretty flowers are?

○ Are these flowers pretty?

○ These flowers pretty are?

7. The sun is hot.

○ Is the sun hot?

○ Hot the sun is?

○ Hot is the sun?

8. The bus is coming.

○ Coming is the bus?

○ The bus coming is?

○ Is the bus coming?

9. Vincent will read this book.

○ Vincent this book will read?

○ Will Vincent read this book?

○ This book will Vincent read?

10. She is my friend.

○ My friend she is?

○ She my friend is?

○ Is she my friend?

Stop

Mathematics

PRACTICE 15 • Measurement

1:30   6:10   2:30   3:55
○   ○   ○   ○

Tips and Reminders

• Listen carefully and look at the picture.

• Look at every answer choice. Then choose an answer.

PRACTICE

1.

4¢   17¢   32¢   37¢
○   ○   ○   ○

2.

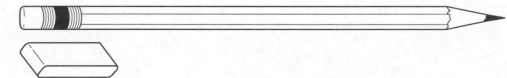

6   5   4   3
○   ○   ○   ○

Go On

3.

1	2	3	4
○	○	○	○

4.

1	2	3	4
○	○	○	○

5.

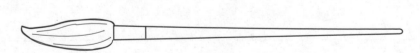

4	10	11	12
○	○	○	○

Go On →

6.

$2.55	$2.30	$1.30	$1.15
○	○	○	○

7.

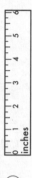

○   ○   ○   ○

8.

○   ○   ○   ○

Stop

59

Reading

Samples

A. Leah's baby sister is <u>tiny</u>.

- ○ hungry
- ○ wet
- ○ quiet
- ○ little

B. Did I <u>fool</u> you?

- ○ stop
- ○ trick
- ○ hear
- ○ find

Tips and Reminders

- Choose the word that best fits in the sentence. Try each answer choice.

PRACTICE

1. Please <u>hand</u> me an apple.

- ○ cook
- ○ take
- ○ give
- ○ bite

2. Max <u>shut</u> the door.

- ○ closed
- ○ opened
- ○ stayed
- ○ pushed

3. Fish swim in the <u>ocean</u>.

- ○ park
- ○ lake
- ○ sea
- ○ rain

4. I <u>own</u> a blue bike.

- ○ have
- ○ ride
- ○ park
- ○ lost

Stop

Sample

C. to <u>start</u>

- ○ begin
- ○ end
- ○ grow
- ○ turn

7. a <u>stone</u>

- ○ flower
- ○ cloud
- ○ rock
- ○ kite

5. is <u>glad</u>

- ○ good
- ○ beautiful
- ○ happy
- ○ mean

8. will <u>shout</u>

- ○ sing
- ○ talk
- ○ cry
- ○ yell

6. a small <u>shop</u>

- ○ room
- ○ store
- ○ picture
- ○ window

9. is <u>below</u>

- ○ under
- ○ around
- ○ over
- ○ near

Stop

Sample

D. Tim heard a _____ outside his window. His cat wanted to come inside.

○ sound

○ bark

○ word

○ rock

12. Tara _____ her room. She put away all her toys.

○ smelled

○ cleaned

○ filled

○ missed

10. The _____ has stopped. The sun is shining, but the grass is still wet.

○ cloud

○ bus

○ rain

○ wind

13. I can't tell you where Scott is. It's a _____.

○ secret

○ letter

○ story

○ song

11. Mom told us to be _____. The baby was sleeping.

○ funny

○ sorry

○ alone

○ quiet

14. Dad made _____ this morning. He cooked eggs for everyone.

○ dinner

○ lunch

○ breakfast

○ noise

Stop

Language Arts

PRACTICE 17 • Writing Paragraphs

Samples

> Matty and his dad went to the zoo. Just as they got there, it began to rain. The animals did not like to get wet. They went into their homes and stayed there.

A. Which of these would go <u>best</u> after the last sentence?

- ○ There were lions and tigers at the zoo.
- ○ Matty's dad works in the city.
- ○ Matty and his dad did not see many animals.

B. Why was this story written?

- ○ To make people laugh
- ○ To tell about a trip to the zoo
- ○ To tell about rain

Tips and Reminders

- Every sentence should fit what the story is mostly about.

- Look at all the answer choices before you choose an answer.

Go On

PRACTICE

Story 1

At night you can the stars see. Some stars together look like pictures in the sky. The Big Dipper is one such sky picture. It looks like a cup with a long handle. Four stars make up the cup. Three stars make the handle.

1. Why was this story written?

○ To tell what the sky looks like

○ To tell about the Big Dipper

○ To tell a sad story about stars

2. What is the <u>best</u> way to write the first sentence?

○ At night you can see the stars.

○ At night the stars can you see.

○ The way it is

Story 2

Alexi likes to spend the night at Grandma's house. First she helps Grandma cook dinner. After dinner, Grandma tells Alexi a story. Sometimes they sing a song together. Then Alexi goes to bed.

3. What is the <u>best</u> way to write the first sentence?

○ The night Alexi likes to spend at Grandma's house.

○ Alexi at Grandma's house likes to spend the night.

○ The way it is

4. Which of these would go <u>best</u> after the last sentence?

○ Alexi likes to eat.

○ Children should not go to bed too late.

○ Alexi always has fun at Grandma's house.

Go On →

Story 3

A mother sea turtle comes out of the sea. She is ready to lay her eggs. She digs a deep hole in the sand. She is making a nest. The sea turtle lays her eggs inside this nest. Then she covers the eggs with sand.

---

5. Which of these would go <u>best</u> after the last sentence?

○ The sand will keep the eggs warm.

○ Sea turtles live in the sea.

○ Some animals like to eat the sea turtle's eggs.

6. Why was this story written?

○ To tell what sea turtles look like

○ To tell what sea turtles eat

○ To tell about a sea turtle laying her eggs

Story 4

Jill a paper kite made one day. She took the kite outside. Soon the wind began to blow. Jill held the kite up over her head. The wind came and blew it high up in the sky.

---

7. Why was this story written?

○ To tell tell how to make a kite

○ To tell about something Jill did

○ To tell about the wind

8. What is the <u>best</u> way to write the first sentence?

○ Jill made a paper kite one day.

○ Jill a paper kite one day made.

○ The way it is

Mathematics

PRACTICE 18 • Addition

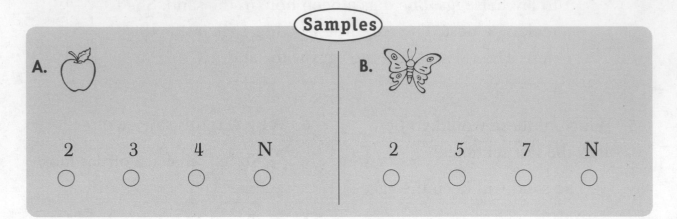

A.

2	3	4	N
○	○	○	○

B.

2	5	7	N
○	○	○	○

Tips and Reminders

- Listen carefully.
- Check your work.

PRACTICE

1.

0	10	12	N
○	○	○	○

3.

8	14	16	N
○	○	○	○

2.

7	12	15	N
○	○	○	○

4.

31	40	41	N
○	○	○	○

Go On ➤

5.
$$2$$
$$+\,4$$

5   6   7   N
○   ○   ○   ○

9.
$$4 + 8 + 3 =$$

12   14   18   N
○   ○   ○   ○

6.
$$4 + 13 =$$

9   17   27   N
○   ○   ○   ○

10.
$$34$$
$$+\,17$$

23   41   51   N
○   ○   ○   ○

7.
$$6$$
$$3$$
$$+\,2$$

11   12   13   N
○   ○   ○   ○

11.
$$6 + 0 =$$

0   6   60   N
○   ○   ○   ○

8.
$$18$$
$$+\,21$$

19   27   39   N
○   ○   ○   ○

12.
$$25$$
$$+\,3$$

19   22   28   N
○   ○   ○   ○

Stop

Reading

PRACTICE 19 • Listening

A.

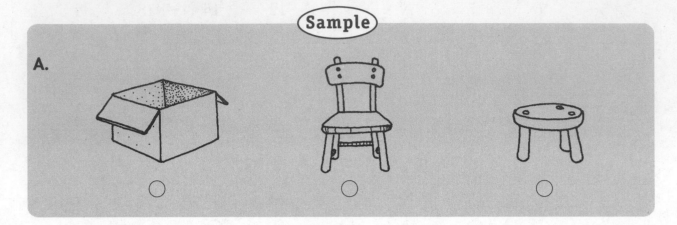

○   ○   ○

Tips and Reminders

- Listen carefully to the story.
- Look at all the answer choices before you choose an answer.

PRACTICE

1.

      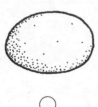

○   ○   ○

2.

○   ○   ○

Go On

68

3.

   ○   ○   ○

4.

   ○   ○   ○

5.

   ○   ○   ○

6.

   ○   ○   ○

Stop

Sample

B.

○ Tipper

○ Mal

○ Andrew

7.

○ "A Big Dog"

○ "The Yellow Duck"

○ "Hide-and-Seek"

8.

○ He saw the dog's tail.

○ The dog barked.

○ The duck quacked.

9.

○ A duck quacked.

○ A goat talked.

○ A dog stood behind some hay.

10.

○ "All About Caves"

○ "Lisa's Mother"

○ "Lisa Visits a Cave"

11.

○ It was snowing.

○ The cave would be cold.

○ It was July.

12.

○ scared

○ angry

○ happy

13.

○ Mom turned on the light.

○ Mom gave Lisa a hug.

○ Lisa walked into the cave.

14.

○ Lisa will run to the car.

○ Dad will come to the cave.

○ Mom will go into the cave.

Stop

Language Arts

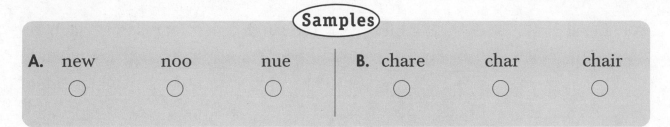

Samples

A. new   noo   nue   **B.** chare   char   chair
○   ○   ○   ○   ○   ○

Tips and Reminders
- Look at all the answer choices.
- Choose the one that looks right.

PRACTICE

1. gon   gan   gone   **5.** store   storry   story
○   ○   ○   ○   ○   ○

2. tabel   table   tabble   **6.** hapy   happey   happy
○   ○   ○   ○   ○   ○

3. floor   flor   flore   **7.** little   litle   littel
○   ○   ○   ○   ○   ○

4. gren   green   grene   **8.** watter   watur   water
○   ○   ○   ○   ○   ○

Go On

9. anmal   animal   animel   15. muther   mother   mothr

  ◯   ◯   ◯   ◯   ◯   ◯

10. berd   bird   birt   16. laugh   laf   lagh

  ◯   ◯   ◯

11. pretty   prity   perty   17. maibe   maybee   maybe

12. wich   wihs   wish   18. childern   children   chilldren

13. white   whit   wite   19. trn   turn   tirn

14. showt   shout   shuot   20. awy   awey   away

Stop

Mathematics

PRACTICE 21 • Subtraction

A.
$$
\begin{array}{r}
12 \\
- 2 \\
\end{array}
$$

8	9	10	N
○	○	○	○

B.
$$
\begin{array}{r}
18 \\
- 11 \\
\end{array}
$$

6	8	9	N
○	○	○	○

Tips and Reminders

- Do the problem first. Then look at the answers. Check your work.

PRACTICE

1.
$$
\begin{array}{r}
16 \\
- 5 \\
\end{array}
$$

11	12	21	N
○	○	○	○

3.
$$
\begin{array}{r}
49 \\
- 7 \\
\end{array}
$$

42	43	44	N
○	○	○	○

2.
$$
\begin{array}{r}
13 \\
- 3 \\
\end{array}
$$

11	12	16	N
○	○	○	○

4.
$$
\begin{array}{r}
56 \\
- 33 \\
\end{array}
$$

89	32	23	N
○	○	○	○

Go On

5.
$$\begin{array}{r} 25 \\ -\ 4 \\ \hline \end{array}$$

20	22	29	N
○	○	○	○

9.
$$\begin{array}{r} 294 \\ -\ 83 \\ \hline \end{array}$$

202	212	217	N
○	○	○	○

6.
$$\begin{array}{r} 92 \\ -\ 71 \\ \hline \end{array}$$

21	22	23	N
○	○	○	○

10.
$$\begin{array}{r} 86 \\ -\ 23 \\ \hline \end{array}$$

62	63	69	N
○	○	○	○

7.
$$\begin{array}{r} 47 \\ -\ 36 \\ \hline \end{array}$$

71	15	11	N
○	○	○	○

11.
$$\begin{array}{r} 463 \\ -\ 12 \\ \hline \end{array}$$

351	375	451	N
○	○	○	○

8.
$$\begin{array}{r} 38 \\ -\ 5 \\ \hline \end{array}$$

33	34	35	N
○	○	○	○

12.
$$\begin{array}{r} 776 \\ -\ 34 \\ \hline \end{array}$$

436	642	742	N
○	○	○	○

Stop

Reading

PRACTICE 22 • Details

Sample

A.

○ The frog is funny.

○ The book is on the table.

○ A bee is on the flower.

Tips and Reminders

• Listen carefully. Look back at the picture or the story to find the answer to each question.

PRACTICE

1.

○ He hides in the box.

○ He eats his lunch.

○ She is in a store.

2.

○ There are many trees.

○ The house is on a hill.

○ The family has breakfast.

3.

○ The man feeds a pig.

○ The king flies a kite.

○ The man drinks some water.

Stop

Samples

Joe is my friend. Last week, Joe and I went to the park. Joe took a bat. I took a ball. We started to play.

A dog ran up. It took the ball and ran away. I got angry.

"Don't get angry," Joe said. "Here, puppy," he called. The dog came back. "Drop the ball," Joe said. It dropped the ball. "Go home!" Joe said. It went.

"Joe," I said, "you are good with dogs!"

Basketball is a great game. It was first played in our country about 100 years ago.

Some people wanted a game to play inside. They got some old baskets. They put the baskets up on the walls. The teams ran back and forth with a ball. Each team tried to throw the ball into one of the baskets.

In Mexico, over 400 years ago, people played a game like basketball. Each player tried to throw a ball through a stone ring.

B. Where did Joe and his friend go?

○ the pet store

○ Joe's house

○ the park

C. Joe told the dog to drop the _____.

○ shoe

○ bat

○ ball

4. When was basketball first played in our country?

○ 10 years ago

○ 100 years ago

○ 400 years ago

5. In Mexico, people threw a ball into a _____.

○ basket

○ stone ring

○ hole in a wall

Go On

Your Bones and You

Your bones are very important. They are like the walls of a house. They hold your body together.

Bones are very strong. They are also very light. Did you know that your bones are alive? If you break a bone, it can grow together again.

Drinking milk can make your bones strong. Most kids should drink about three cups of milk a day. Some kids cannot drink milk because it makes them sick. They need to ask a doctor about other ways to have strong bones.

6. What happens if you break a bone?

   ○ It stays broken.

   ○ Your body grows a new bone.

   ○ The bone grows together again.

7. How many cups of milk should kids drink each day?

   ○ one

   ○ two

   ○ three

8. Bones are very _____.

   ○ weak

   ○ heavy

   ○ important

9. If you cannot drink milk, you should talk to a _____.

   ○ doctor

   ○ teacher

   ○ cook

Stop

Language Arts

PRACTICE 23 • Punctuation

Samples

A.

- ○ Ann is always cold
- ○ She is cold at school.
- ○ She is cold at home?

B.

- ○ Jill got the bat?
- ○ Did you get the ball?
- ○ Now we can play

Tips and Reminders

- Check each punctuation mark.
- A telling sentence ends with a period. An asking sentence ends with a question mark (?).

PRACTICE

1.

- ○ We have a new car.
- ○ The car is red
- ○ Is your car red.

3.

- ○ Jim has a funny book.
- ○ It is about a mouse?
- ○ Did you read that book

2.

- ○ That lunch was nice
- ○ Now I want an apple?
- ○ May I have one?

4.

- ○ Kate fell down
- ○ Her leg is black and blue.
- ○ Did she cry

Go On →

5.
- ○ How was that TV show?
- ○ Was it about tigers
- ○ How long was it.

6.
- ○ Willie picked a flower
- ○ Why did he pick it.
- ○ He gave it to his mom.

7.
- ○ A clown came to school
- ○ She made funny faces?
- ○ She made me laugh.

8.
- ○ Where is my father.
- ○ Is he in the room?
- ○ He is cooking lunch

9.
- ○ Who will paint the house.
- ○ The worker will paint it
- ○ She will paint it yellow.

10.
- ○ That rabbit is small?
- ○ The rabbit hops.
- ○ Will it come close to us.

11.
- ○ Who is that man
- ○ He is the mayor?
- ○ He lives on my street.

12.
- ○ Nick went to the lake.
- ○ There was a big rock
- ○ Did he stand on the rock.

13.
- ○ A letter came for me
- ○ Where did you put it?
- ○ Is it on the table.

14.
- ○ Emmy has a funny pet
- ○ Her pet is a pig?
- ○ It eats a lot of food.

Stop

Mathematics

PRACTICE 24 • Charts and Graphs

Samples

March

Sunday	Monday	Tuesday	Wednesday	Thursday	Friday	Saturday
	1	2	3	4	5	6
7	8	9	10	11	12	13
14	15	16	17	18	19	20
21	22	23	24	25	26	27
28	29	30	31			

A.
5 ○ 6 ○ 7 ○ 8 ○

B.
Monday ○   Tuesday ○   Wednesday ○   Thursday ○

Tips and Reminders

• Use the picture to answer each question.

• Look at every answer choice before you choose an answer.

Go On

PRACTICE

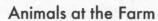

Animals at the Farm

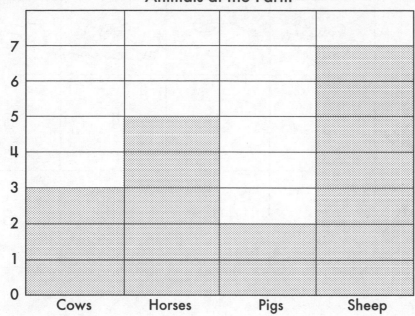

1.   Horses   Cows   Pigs   Sheep
       ◯   ◯   ◯   ◯

---

2.   2   3   6   7
       ◯   ◯   ◯   ◯

---

3.   Horses   Cows   Pigs   Sheep
       ◯   ◯   ◯   ◯

---

4.   2   3   4   5
       ◯   ◯   ◯   ◯

Go On →

Stuffed Animal Toys

	Bears	Bunnies	Cats	Dogs
Tracy	6	1	4	5
Amy	7	2	1	3

5.

2	3	4	7
○	○	○	○

6.

Bears	Bunnies	Cats	Dogs
○	○	○	○

7.

9	10	13	16
○	○	○	○

8.

4	5	6	7
○	○	○	○

Reading

PRACTICE 25 • Understanding Text

Samples

How does Mike get ready?

Mike is a circus clown. Before each show, he puts on his clown face. First he covers his face with a white paste. Next he paints on a huge orange smile. He draws lines around his eyes. Then he puts on a tiny purple hat. Mike wants to look funny, and he does!

A. What does Mike put on first?

- ○ an orange smile
- ○ white paste
- ○ lines around his eyes

B. What is this story mostly about?

- ○ how Mike puts on his clown face
- ○ going to the circus
- ○ why Mike likes being a clown

Tips and Reminders

- Look back at the story to find answers.
- Look for signal words, such as *first, next, then,* and *because.*

PRACTICE

What do moths look like?

Many moths are beautiful. But they come out at night. How can you see what they look like? There is a way!

First, make some moth food. Start with two cups of orange juice. Pour it into a bowl. Add two really soft bananas. Then spoon in some honey. Mix everything together. Last, cover the bowl and leave it in the sun for a few hours.

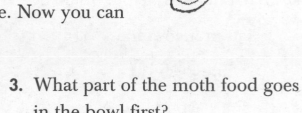

When the moth food is ready, take it outside. Bring an old cloth, too. Use the cloth to spread some moth food on a tree. Later, go back out after dark. Bring a light with you. Shine it on the tree. You will probably see some moths enjoying the food you made. Now you can watch them up close.

1. This story is mainly about —

   ○ the names of moths

   ○ how to watch moths

   ○ where moths live

2. Why is it hard to get a good look at moths?

   ○ They fly so fast.

   ○ They are very small.

   ○ They come out at night.

3. What part of the moth food goes in the bowl first?

   ○ honey

   ○ bananas

   ○ orange juice

4. Which step comes last?

   ○ Shine a light on the tree.

   ○ Bring an old cloth.

   ○ Spread moth food on a tree.

Making a Rainbow

The first graders wanted to paint a rainbow. Their teacher taped a big piece of paper on the wall. Then she took out blue, red, and yellow paints.

"We need more paint!" the children said. "We need green and orange and purple."

The teacher smiled. "You can make those colors by mixing red, blue, and yellow," she said. "Try it."

Tori mixed red and yellow. "I made orange!" she said. Harry mixed yellow and blue to make green. Then Donna said, "I mixed red and blue. They made purple."

Finally, Tommy said, "I mixed red and blue and yellow all together. They made brown." The other children laughed. They did not need brown for their rainbow.

---

5. What happened first?

○ The children painted a rainbow.

○ The teacher cut some paper.

○ Tori mixed red and yellow.

6. When Harry mixed yellow and blue, he made —

○ red

○ purple

○ green

7. Why did the children laugh at Tommy?

○ He got paint on his face.

○ He made brown.

○ He did not like rainbows.

8. What is this story mostly about?

○ A teacher cut some paper.

○ Some children mixed colors to paint a rainbow.

○ Donna made purple.

Does Dan feel okay?

Today Dan is going to see Dr. Wayans. But Dan is not sick. He goes to the doctor once each year. Dr. Wayans wants to make sure he is fine.

First Dr. Wayans finds out how much Dan has grown. Next she uses a special tool to look inside his ears. She looks inside his mouth, too. With another tool, she listens to his heart. So far, everything is fine.

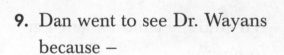

Finally, Dr. Wayans tests Dan's eyes. She points to the letters on the wall. He tries to read them. But he has a little trouble. Dr. Wayans thinks Dan might need glasses. She will send Dan to Dr. Billings. Dr. Billings knows all about eyes.

9. Dan went to see Dr. Wayans because –

○ she wanted to make sure he was fine

○ he felt sick

○ he could not hear well

10. What did Dr. Wayans do first?

○ looked in Dan's mouth

○ listened to Dan's heart

○ found out how much Dan had grown

11. Dan will go to see Dr. Billings because –

○ his heart sounds weak

○ he may need glasses

○ his ears hurt

12. What is the best title for this story?

○ "Visiting the Doctor"

○ "How Your Eyes Work"

○ "Dan Gets Sick"

Language Arts

PRACTICE 26 • Capitalization

Samples

A.
- ○ Dina and i are ready for
- ○ lunch. We have some bread
- ○ and cheese for sandwiches.

B.
- ○ Tina will go to school
- ○ in september. She will ride on
- ○ the big yellow school bus.

Tips and Reminders

- Each sentence should begin with a capital letter.
- Capitalize the names of people, pets, days, and months.

PRACTICE

1.
- ○ This green bike belongs
- ○ to my sister kate. She rides it
- ○ to work almost every day.

2.
- ○ Dad just came back from
- ○ the store. He saw mrs. Levine
- ○ and her new baby.

3.
- ○ Do you have enough
- ○ money for the train? the
- ○ ticket costs five dollars.

4.
- ○ We sent a card to our
- ○ teacher, Mr. Harris. He has
- ○ been sick since wednesday.

Go On →

5.

- ○ Kim saw an odd bump in
- ○ the bed. His cat boots was
- ○ sleeping under the blanket.

6.

- ○ This is where dr. Renaldo
- ○ works. She takes care of cows,
- ○ sheep, and other animals.

7.

- ○ My neighbor has many
- ○ trees. In the fall, i help her
- ○ rake the leaves in her yard.

8.

- ○ Every saturday morning,
- ○ my brother and his friends
- ○ play basketball in the park.

9.

- ○ The duggans live in the
- ○ last house on the street. They
- ○ moved in a few weeks ago.

10.

- ○ Lisa can hardly wait until
- ○ january. That is when she will
- ○ be in the school play.

11.

- ○ Dad says two friends may
- ○ sleep over at our house. But
- ○ first i have to clean my room.

12.

- ○ Cats and dogs make Mom
- ○ sneeze. But she does not
- ○ mind my pet snake, benny.

Stop

Mathematics

PRACTICE 27 • Solving Problems

Sample

$7 - 3 = 4$ ◯

$4 + 3 = 7$ ◯

$10 + 3 = 13$ ◯

$4 - 3 = 1$ ◯

Tips and Reminders

• Listen carefully to the question.

• Look at every answer choice before choosing an answer.

PRACTICE

1.

$5 - 1 = 4$ ◯

$6 + 1 = 7$ ◯

$5 + 1 = 6$ ◯

$6 - 5 = 1$ ◯

2.

$14 - 8 = 6$ ◯

$9 + 5 = 14$ ◯

$14 + 8 = 22$ ◯

$14 - 5 = 9$ ◯

Go On →

3.

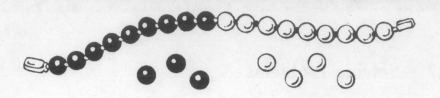

$$9 + 7 = 16 \qquad 9 - 7 = 2 \qquad 9 + 9 = 18 \qquad 18 - 9 = 9$$
◯ ◯ ◯ ◯

4.

$$11 - 3 = 8 \qquad 14 - 8 = 6 \qquad 3 + 11 = 14 \qquad 14 - 3 = 11$$
◯ ◯ ◯ ◯

5.

$$9 - 5 = 4 \qquad 14 - 9 = 5 \qquad 14 + 5 = 19 \qquad 9 + 5 = 14$$
◯ ◯ ◯ ◯

6.

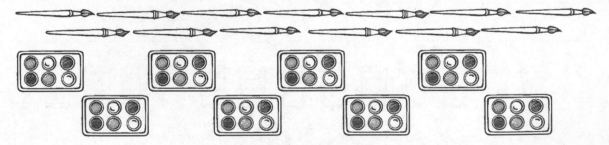

$$8 + 6 = 14 \qquad 13 + 6 = 19 \qquad 13 - 8 = 5 \qquad 13 - 6 = 7$$
◯ ◯ ◯ ◯

Stop

Reading

Samples

Sink or Float

Salim did a trick for his friends. He started with two glasses and two eggs. He dropped one egg into a glass. It sank to the bottom.

"Of course," said Joe. "Everyone knows an egg won't float."

"Don't be so sure," said Salim. He put the other egg into the other glass. It sank. But then it slowly floated to the top.

"How did you do that?" asked Joe. Macy knew. She took the floating egg out of the glass. Then she had Joe sip the water. He made a face and said, "Oh! That water is salty!"

"That's right," said Macy. "An egg will float in salty water."

A. What was different about the second glass of water?

○ It was very cold.

○ It was almost empty.

○ It was very salty.

B. How did Joe feel when he sipped the water?

○ surprised

○ worried

○ glad

Tips and Reminders

• Read the story carefully.

• Look for clues in the story to help answer the questions.

Go On

PRACTICE

Looking for Binky

Ann's cousin Jeff was visiting for two days. Ann showed Jeff around the house. Then she said, "Come see my pet rabbit." She led Jeff to Binky's cage.

"Let's let him out," Jeff said.

But Ann told Jeff that Binky was not like a cat. "He doesn't like to wander. His cage keeps him from getting scared or hurt," she said.

The next morning, Binky's cage was empty. Ann and Mom looked everywhere for him. Ann found him under a chair. Binky looked sick.

Mom pointed to her plant. "Binky ate most of it," she said. "That's why he is sick. We'll have to take him to the vet."

Jeff heard what Mom said. He felt bad. "I just thought Binky should have a chance to hop around," he said.

---

1. How is Binky different from a dog or cat?

   ○ He is not a friendly pet.

   ○ He doesn't like to wander.

   ○ He likes to go outside.

2. Who let Binky out of his cage?

   ○ Mom

   ○ Ann

   ○ Jeff

3. Jeff felt bad at the end of the story because –

   ○ Binky was sick

   ○ it was time to go home

   ○ the plant was gone

4. What will Binky do next?

   ○ go to the vet

   ○ eat some rabbit food

   ○ get a new cage

Bad Luck for Dad

Dad looked out the window. "It's a bad day for Pilar to walk to school," he said. "I will drive her in the car."

Soon Dad and Pilar were driving toward school. But then the car began to slow down. "Oh, no," said Dad. "We have run out of gas." He pulled the car to the side of the road.

Dad and Pilar got out of the car. They started walking. Pilar carried her little umbrella. But Dad did not have an umbrella. By the time they got to Pilar's school, Dad's clothes were wet.

Dad said goodbye to Pilar. She watched him walk out of the school. His wet clothes left a trail of water on the floor. Pilar felt sorry for Dad.

---

5. What was the weather like outside?

○ It was sunny.

○ It was raining.

○ It was windy.

7. How was Pilar different from Dad in this story?

○ She got wet.

○ She liked to walk.

○ She stayed dry.

---

6. Dad was trying to be –

○ helpful

○ bossy

○ funny

8. What will happen next?

○ Pilar will walk home.

○ Dad will get gas for the car.

○ Pilar will get an umbrella.

Mrs. Lee's New Book

Mrs. Lee writes books for children. Her books are about Kay. Kay is six years old. She has red hair. Funny things happen to Kay in Mrs. Lee's books.

Kay is a lot like Mrs. Lee's neighbor. Her name is Becca. Becca is six, like Kay. Her hair is red, like Kay's. When something funny happens to Becca, Mrs. Lee wants to know.

Becca visited Mrs. Lee yesterday. "Something funny happened," she said. "I was eating an apple. I took a big bite. I felt my tooth come out. But I could not find my tooth anywhere."

Mrs. Lee laughed at Becca's story. She thanked Becca for visiting her. And today Mrs. Lee is very busy. She is writing a new book about Kay.

9. What happened to Becca's tooth?

- ◯ It fell out.
- ◯ She gave it away.
- ◯ Mrs. Lee took it.

10. How does Mrs. Lee feel when Becca visits?

- ◯ worried
- ◯ glad
- ◯ tired

11. How is Kay like Becca?

- ◯ She lives next to Mrs. Lee.
- ◯ Her hair is brown.
- ◯ Funny things happen to her.

12. What will Mrs. Lee's new book be about?

- ◯ Kay moves away.
- ◯ Kay picks some apples.
- ◯ Kay loses a tooth.

Language Arts

Sample

Time to Eat

A. Where should you start reading to learn how to make sandwiches?

○ page 18

○ page 25

○ page 32

B. Which pages would tell most about buying the right foods?

○ pages 3–10

○ pages 11–17

○ pages 25–31

Tips and Reminders

• Listen for key words to help you answer each question.

• To put words in A-B-C order, look at the first letter in each word.

PRACTICE

The Firefighter's Job

1. Where should you start reading to find out about a firefighter's clothes?

   ○ page 2

   ○ page 9

   ○ page 14

2. Which pages would tell most about where firefighters sleep and eat?

   ○ pages 14–22

   ○ pages 23–27

   ○ pages 28–34

3. Which pages would tell most about the axes and hoses that firefighters use?

   ○ pages 9–13

   ○ pages 14–22

   ○ pages 28–34

4. Where should you start reading to find out what happens when there is a fire?

   ○ page 2

   ○ page 14

   ○ page 35

Go On

5. Which picture should come first?

○ Dish

○ Apple

○ Fish

6. Which picture should come between Carrot and Egg?

○ Dish

○ Beet

○ Glass

7. Which picture should be right before Fish?

○ Beet

○ Glass

○ Egg

8. Which picture should be last?

○ Glass

○ Apple

○ Carrot

Stop

Mathematics

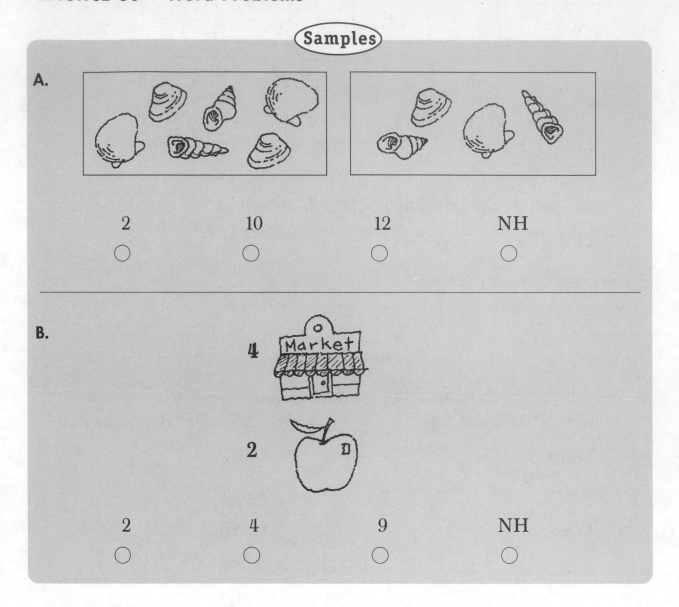

Samples

A.

2   10   12   NH
○   ○   ○   ○

B.

4 Market

2 🍎

2   4   9   NH
○   ○   ○   ○

Go On

PRACTICE

1.

11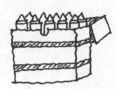

7

4	16	18	NH
○	○	○	○

2.

$8

$3

$5	$11	$14	NH
○	○	○	○

3.

4    3

1	7	9	NH
○	○	○	○

Go On →

4.

10¢

25¢

15¢	25¢	35¢	NH
○	○	○	○

5.

36

7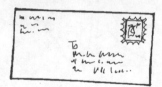

27	30	43	NH
○	○	○	○

6.

2  6

4	8	12	NH
○	○	○	○

Stop

READING: Sounds and Letters

Sample

A.

pan   not   map   for

○   ○   ○   ○

1.

spot   moon   tooth   fast

○   ○   ○   ○

2.

send   next   sun   zoo

○   ○   ○   ○

Sample

B.

man   fun   food   them

○   ○   ○   ○

3.

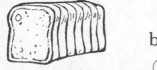

ball   sad   hat   bring

○   ○   ○   ○

Go On

4.

train   her   start   ran
○   ○   ○   ○

5.

bath   out   thin   hot
○   ○   ○   ○

Sample

C.

trip   hit   neck   shop
○   ○   ○   ○

6.

pets   hop   coat   said
○   ○   ○   ○

7.

fill   tie   pan   log
○   ○   ○   ○

8.

fell   let   field   off
○   ○   ○   ○

Stop

Post-test

READING: Vocabulary

Sample

A.	song	cloud	park	boat
	○	○	○	○

1.	noise	window	mouse	lion
	○	○	○	○

2.	please	first	bite	yell
	○	○	○	○

3.	sad	pretty	tonight	paint
	○	○	○	○

4.	under	again	surprise	sometime
	○	○	○	○

5.	grass	cake	rope	tire
	○	○	○	○

Stop

Sample

B. Jan did not mean to drop the cup. She is _____.

○ glad

○ last

○ sorry

8. It is almost time to go to school. The _____ will be here soon.

○ lunch

○ bus

○ bird

6. The sky is getting very dark. Soon it will be _____.

○ yellow

○ well

○ black

9. The baby is asleep. Everyone should be _____.

○ quiet

○ small

○ more

7. I lost my toy train. I _____ I could get a new one.

○ wish

○ cook

○ walk

10. It snowed all night. We will not go to school _____.

○ until

○ today

○ ever

Stop

Post-test

READING: Comprehension

Samples

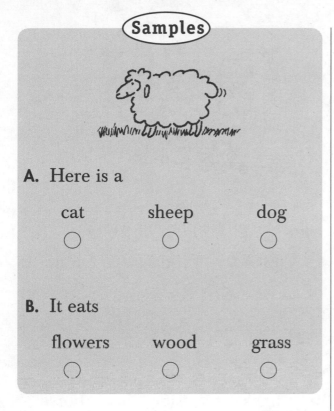

A. Here is a

    cat   sheep   dog

    ○   ○   ○

B. It eats

    flowers   wood   grass

    ○   ○   ○

1. Min pays with

    nothing   tricks   money

    ○   ○   ○

2. Min is getting a toy

    boat   truck   house

    ○   ○   ○

3. The teacher is

    reading   drawing   sleeping

    ○   ○   ○

4. The children are on the

    table   water   floor

    ○   ○   ○

Go On

5. Alex is with his

    mom   dad   brother

    ○   ○   ○

8. The girl is playing with a

    bike   boat   train

    ○   ○   ○

6. They are

    walking   washing   cooking

    ○   ○   ○

9. It is on a

    track   store   horse

    ○   ○   ○

7. The food goes into a

    rock   pot   bus

    ○   ○   ○

10. It goes by a

    house   laugh   book

    ○   ○   ○

Stop

Samples

Grandma

Grandma went for a swim. She went in the lake. The water was very cold. Grandma was cold when she got out. She walked home. She had a hot drink.

C. The water in the lake was

- ○ hot
- ○ cold
- ○ not clean

D. What did Grandma do last?

- ○ went home
- ○ went for a swim
- ○ drank something hot

The Big Cats

There are seven kinds of big cats. Two of them are lions and tigers. Tigers are the biggest cats. Lions are almost as big. Lions live in big families. Tigers live alone most of the time. Most big cats do not like water. But tigers like to go in water.

11. How many kinds of big cats are there?

- ○ two
- ○ five
- ○ seven

12. Lions are not like tigers because they

- ○ are big cats
- ○ live in families
- ○ like water

Going to the Party

Amber and her mother got into the car.
Mom was taking Amber to a birthday party.

A big truck pulled in front of them. It was slow.
It was painting a yellow line down the road.

"Let's try a new way to Ann's house,"
said Amber's mother.

She turned one way. Then she turned
another way.

"Oh, no," she said. "Now I am lost."

"Look!" said Amber. "There is Ann's house
up ahead!"

13. What did Amber do first?

○ She saw a truck.

○ She got into the car.

○ She saw Ann's house.

14. Where were Amber and her
mother going?

○ to a party

○ to a shop

○ to their house

15. Why did Amber's mother try a
new way to Ann's house?

○ She did not want to stay
behind the truck.

○ She was tired of going the
same old way.

○ She wanted to get lost.

16. What will Amber's mother do
next?

○ look for the truck

○ get a birthday toy for Ann

○ go up to Ann's house

READING: Listening

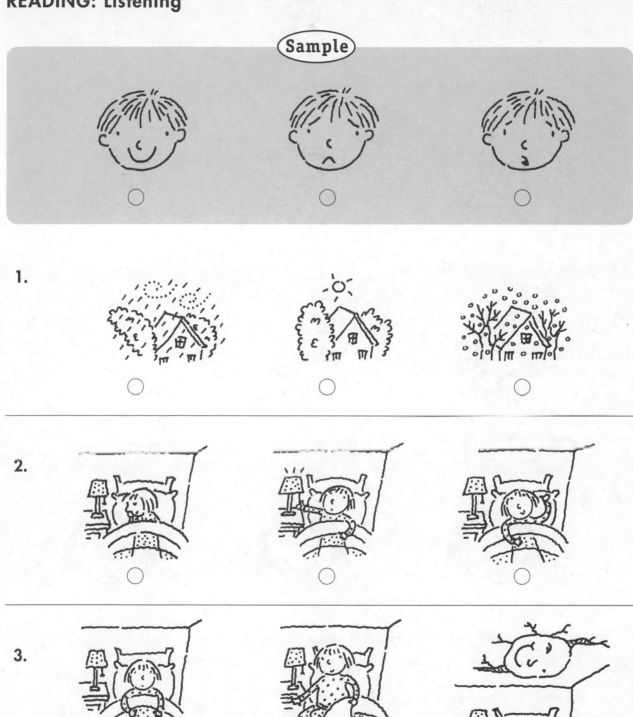

4.

○ ○ ○

5.

○ ○ ○

6.

○ ○ ○

7.

○ ○ ○

8.

○ ○ ○ **Stop**

Post-test

LANGUAGE ARTS: Usage

Sample

A. My house _____.

- ○ is here
- ○ and your house
- ○ in the town

1. Mom _____ it was time to go.

- ○ say
- ○ saying
- ○ said

2. Russ got two _____.

- ○ prize
- ○ prizes

3. All the people _____.

- ○ in the yard
- ○ watched the show
- ○ on the farm

4. _____ in the lake.

- ○ Lots of fish
- ○ A little puppy
- ○ Jan jumped

5. That is the _____ cake I have ever seen!

- ○ big
- ○ bigger
- ○ biggest

6. The teacher _____ that book.

- ○ likes
- ○ like

7. My brother took my coat because _____ was cold.

- ○ he
- ○ she
- ○ they

Stop

Sample

B. The balloon is red.

○ Red is the balloon?

○ Is red the balloon?

○ Is the balloon red?

Sample

C. ○ The children on their bikes.

○ Riding down the road.

○ They had a good time.

---

8. I can draw.

○ Can I draw?

○ Draw I can?

○ I draw can?

11. ○ The circus is coming.

○ Clowns with funny faces.

○ Can't wait to go!

---

9. Dan will get stuck.

○ Get stuck will Dan?

○ Will Dan get stuck?

○ Dan stuck will get?

12. ○ Made some cookies.

○ Then we ate them.

○ With a glass of milk.

---

10. The baby is laughing.

○ Laughing is the baby?

○ Is baby the laughing?

○ Is the baby laughing?

13. ○ The big, yellow bus.

○ It takes the kids to school.

○ Stopping by my house.

Stop

Post-test

LANGUAGE ARTS: Mechanics

Sample

A.
- ○   Aunt Susan took a
- ○ trip. she went on a big
- ○ boat across the sea.

1.
- ○   Kate missed school
- ○ on tuesday. She was sick
- ○ and went to the doctor.

2.
- ○   Mike and i fed an
- ○ apple to the horse. Then
- ○ we played in the barn.

3.
- ○   what is the name of
- ○ that song? You and your
- ○ sister Jane sing it.

4.
- ○   We played a game in
- ○ the garden. We tried to
- ○ catch Jim and tom.

5.
- ○   Helen will paint our
- ○ house yellow. She will
- ○ start work on march 12.

Stop

Sample

B.

- ○ Flowers grow in spring
- ○ These flowers smell good?
- ○ I will water the garden.

Sample

C.

please   coler   was
○   ○   ○

6.

- ○ Where is the cat.
- ○ Did she run after a mouse?
- ○ I'm glad the mouse got away

7.

- ○ I just lost my kite?
- ○ It flew into a tree
- ○ I cannot get it down.

8.

- ○ Do you like cake?
- ○ My dad just baked one
- ○ Let's each have some?

9.

always   appel   before
○   ○   ○

10.

should   wait   family
○   ○   ○

11.

snak   road   morning
○   ○   ○

12.

give   book   furst
○   ○   ○

Stop

Post-test

LANGUAGE ARTS: Writing

Sample

A. I got some milk to drink.
The milk fell on the floor.

_____

○ I like milk.

○ I cleaned up the milk.

○ Mom had some milk, too.

---

1. Pete got money for his birthday.
Dad took Pete to the toy store.

_____

○ Pete got a new toy.

○ Pete's birthday is in June.

○ Pete loves books.

---

2. Zack was riding his bike.
Zack came to a big hill.

_____

○ Zack's bike is new.

○ Where is that hill?

○ Zack rode up slowly.

Grandpa took us to the park.
There was a small lake there.
We sailed a toy boat in it.
Then we felt hot.
We wanted something to drink.

_____

3. ○ The lake was so pretty.

○ Grandpa got some cold
drinks for us.

○ The boat had a white sail.

4. ○ to tell about a trip to the park

○ to make you laugh

○ to tell you how to make a toy
boat

Stop

Sample

B.

- ⚪ ask
- ⚪ cry
- ⚪ best

6.

- ⚪ pound
- ⚪ dark
- ⚪ face

5.

- ⚪ never
- ⚪ sound
- ⚪ keep

7.

- ⚪ yet
- ⚪ zoo
- ⚪ tire

Contents

8.

- ⚪ page 6
- ⚪ page 11
- ⚪ page 18

9.

- ⚪ Birds
- ⚪ Kittens
- ⚪ Dogs

Stop

116

Post-test

MATHEMATICS: Concepts

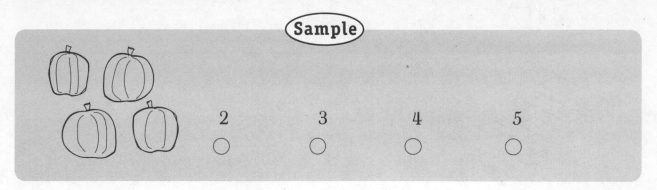

Sample

2 ○   3 ○   4 ○   5 ○

1.

○   ○   ○   ○

2.

○   ○   ○   ○

3.

309 ○   93 ○   39 ○   30 ○

4.

| 8 |

two ○   six ○   four ○   eight ○

Go On →

117

5.

      5   9   6   4

      ◯   ◯   ◯   ◯

6.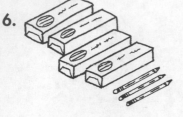

      43   33   34   40

      ◯   ◯   ◯   ◯

7.

  24   25   21   22

  ◯   ◯   ◯   ◯

8.

6	8		12	14

  9   11   16   10

  ◯   ◯   ◯   ◯

9.

    ◯   ◯   ◯   ◯

MATHEMATICS: Concepts (continued)

10.

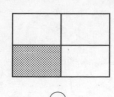 

○   ○   ○   ○

11.

$$5 + 3 = 8$$

$8 + 3 = 11$ $5 + 8 = 13$ $5 - 3 = 2$ $8 - 3 = 5$

○   ○   ○   ○

12.

○   ○   ○   ○

13.

○   ○   ○   ○

14.

 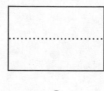

○   ○   ○   ○

Go On →

15.

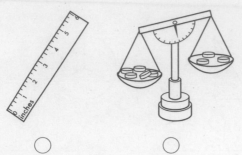 

    ◯   ◯   ◯   ◯

16.

54¢	28¢	63¢	74¢
◯	◯	◯	◯

17.

    ◯   ◯   ◯   ◯

18.

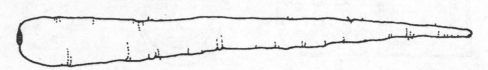

4	6	7	9
◯	◯	◯	◯

Stop

120

Post-test

MATHEMATICS: Computation

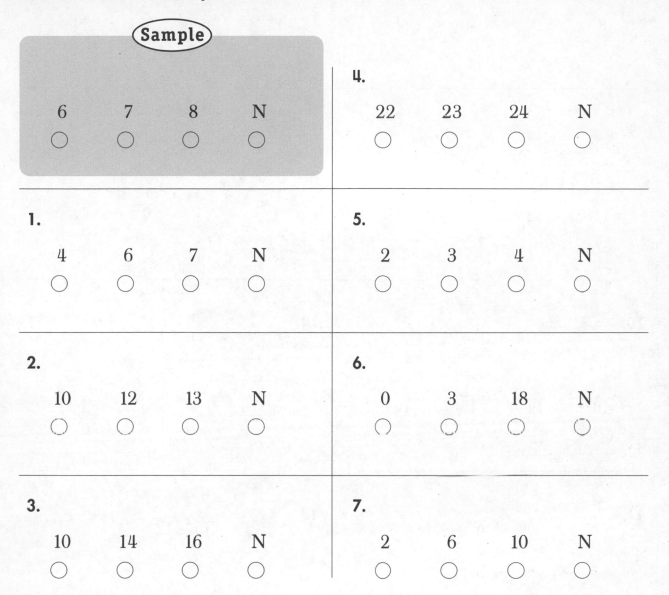

Sample

6	7	8	N
○	○	○	○

4.

22	23	24	N
○	○	○	○

1.

4	6	7	N
○	○	○	○

5.

2	3	4	N
○	○	○	○

2.

10	12	13	N
○	○	○	○

6.

0	3	18	N
○	○	○	○

3.

10	14	16	N
○	○	○	○

7.

2	6	10	N
○	○	○	○

Go On

8.

$$\begin{array}{r} 6 \\ + 4 \\ \hline \end{array}$$

8   9   10   N

○   ○   ○   ○

9.

$$\begin{array}{r} 5 \\ + 9 \\ \hline \end{array}$$

11   12   13   N

○   ○   ○   ○

10.

$$14 + 0 =$$

13   14   15   N

○   ○   ○   ○

11.

$$\begin{array}{r} 6 \\ 7 \\ + 3 \\ \hline \end{array}$$

16   17   19   N

○   ○   ○   ○

12.

$$\begin{array}{r} 34 \\ + 23 \\ \hline \end{array}$$

17   56   57   N

○   ○   ○   ○

13.

$$\begin{array}{r} 7 \\ - 6 \\ \hline \end{array}$$

1   3   4   N

○   ○   ○   ○

14.

$$\begin{array}{r} 13 \\ - 8 \\ \hline \end{array}$$

3   4   6   N

○   ○   ○   ○

15.

$$36 - 12 =$$

24   25   44   N

○   ○   ○   ○

Stop

Post-test

MATHEMATICS: Problem Solving

7   3

10	6	5	4
○	○	○	○

1.

$10 + 6 = \square$	$10 - 6 = \square$	$6 + 10 = \square$	$6 - 10 = \square$
○	○	○	○

2.

3	5	6	7
○	○	○	○

3.

9	13	14	15
○	○	○	○

4.

2	3	4	5
○	○	○	○

Go On →

	4
	2
	8
	3

5.

12	14	16	17
○	○	○	○

6.

○	○	○	○

7.

20	10	8	6
○	○	○	○

8.

PRETZELS 35¢	POTATO CHIPS 50¢	CHEESE AND CRACKERS 65¢	POPCORN 40¢
○	○	○	○

9.

$8	$9	$10	$11
○	○	○	○

10.

45 pounds	46 pounds	47 pounds	48 pounds
○	○	○	○

Stop

124

Scoring Chart

Name _____ Class _____

Directions: Use this page to keep a record of your work. Make a check mark (✔) beside each test you finish. Then write your test score.

✔ PRETEST	Score	%
Reading	/42	
Language Arts	/34	
Mathematics	/43	
Total	/119	

✔ POST-TEST	Score	%
Reading	/42	
Language Arts	/34	
Mathematics	/43	
Total	/119	

✔ PRACTICE TEST	Score	%
1. Letter Sounds	/10	
2. Nouns and Pronouns	/12	
3. Whole Number Concepts	/10	
4. Consonants	/8	
5. Verbs	/12	
6. Counting	/8	
7. Vowels	/8	
8. Adjectives	/12	
9. Using Numbers	/8	
10. Sight Words	/12	
11. Sentences	/8	
12. Shapes	/10	
13. Words and Pictures	/13	
14. Writing Sentences	/10	
15. Measurement	/8	

✔ PRACTICE TEST	Score	%
16. Vocabulary	/14	
17. Writing Paragraphs	/8	
18. Addition	/12	
19. Listening	/14	
20. Spelling	/20	
21. Subtraction	/12	
22. Details	/9	
23. Punctuation	/14	
24. Charts and Graphs	/8	
25. Understanding Text	/12	
26. Capitalization	/12	
27. Solving Problems	/6	
28. Stories	/12	
29. Locating Information	/8	
30. Word Problems	/6	